essential careers™

CAREERS IN WOMEN'S HEALTH

JERI FREEDMAN

Rosen
YA™

New York

Published in 2018 by The Rosen Publishing Group, Inc.
29 East 21st Street, New York, NY 10010

First Edition

Library of Congress Cataloging-in-Publication Data

Names: Freedman, Jeri, author.
Title: Careers in women's health / Jeri Freedman.
Description: New York: Rosen Publishing, 2018. | Series: Essential careers |
Audience: Grades 7–12. | Includes bibliographical references and index.
Identifiers: LCCN 2017016029 | ISBN 9781538381588 (library bound) |
ISBN 9781508178750 (paperback)
Subjects: LCSH: Women in medicine—Juvenile literature. | Medicine—Vocational guidance.
Classification: LCC R692 .F73 2018 | DDC 610.82—dc23
LC record available at https://lccn.loc.gov/2017016029

Manufactured in China

contents

INTRODUCTION   4

CHAPTER 1: HELPING WOMEN STAY HEALTHY   7

CHAPTER 2: PREPARING FOR A WOMEN'S

HEALTH CAREER   18

CHAPTER 3: NURSES IN WOMEN'S HEALTH CARE   25

CHAPTER 4: WOMEN'S DOCTORS   34

CHAPTER 5: DELIVERING BABIES   41

CHAPTER 6: WOMEN'S HEALTH TECHNICAL

AND SUPPORT CAREERS   50

CHAPTER 7: LANDING A JOB AND ADVANCEMENT   60

GLOSSARY   67

FOR MORE INFORMATION   70

FOR FURTHER READING   74

BIBLIOGRAPHY   75

INDEX   77

INTRO

A midwife monitors the health of an unborn child. Such jobs provide the satisfaction of helping mothers and babies.

DUCTION

In the *Telegraph* newspaper article "What Is It Actually Like to Be a Midwife Today?," Caroline Burton, who was named the Midwife of the Year by Johnson Baby Awards in 2014, says of delivering a baby, "It's fantastic. You're there at a really special moment. Usually you're the first person to touch that baby. You're effectively a complete stranger but you're involved in it." A career in women's health can be demanding and may require unpredictable working hours, but it can be extremely fulfilling. It provides the opportunity to help women and improve their health and lives. Some jobs allow one to participate in the unique experience of helping to bring new life into the world. The women's health field encompasses a variety of areas.

Health professionals and researchers have recognized that women's physiology differs from that of men. Diseases such as osteoporosis, fibromyalgia, chronic fatigue, sexual dysfunction, cancer, heart disease, orthopedic injuries, and genetic or age-related disorders have specific effects on women, and women require different diagnosis and treatment approaches than men. Women's health professionals address these issues as well as those related to childbirth and reproductive health.

Programs to improve health for women have grown over the past couple of decades. The growth means that there has been a similar increase in jobs available in the field. Women's health care jobs are secure and pay well, but they offer more than a paycheck. They allow a person to make a difference in the lives of others.

There are a large number of jobs in women's health, and in some locations there is a shortage of people to fill those positions. In addition, demand for most women's health care jobs is expected to increase faster than demand in many other fields. The women's health care field offers jobs for college graduates and for high school graduates with on-the-job or a small amount of training. Many jobs require completing a training program that ranges from a few months to two years. Still others are suitable for those with a four-year college degree. This resource provides information about the activities each type of job entails and the skills, training, and certification required for the job. It also discusses practical ways to successfully locate and apply for a job.

Health care is a "people" profession. For those seeking a career in women's health care, personal qualities may be as important as training. A health care professional is working with members of the public who are unwell and, frequently, with their family members, who are stressed. Employers want to hire people with traits such as empathy, patience, attention to detail, and problem-solving skills. Further, because most health care today is delivered by a team of professionals, one must be able to work well with others.

A variety of changes in demographics have increased the demand for health care. Among these factors are the aging of the population, the fact that millennials are starting to marry and have children, the influence of health insurance companies on the way health care is provided, and an increased number of people being covered by health insurance. These changes have created a tremendous demand for health care workers. Because of this need, jobs are likely to remain plentiful in this field for a long time.

chapter 1

HELPING WOMEN STAY HEALTHY

There are two aspects to women's health. The first is that some ailments are female-specific—related to a woman's reproductive system and childbirth. The second is the fact that diseases and disorders that affect both men and women may affect women differently or to a greater degree than they do men. For instance, the symptoms that women experience when they are having a heart attack are different from those commonly experienced by men.

A HISTORY OF WOMEN'S HEALTH CARE

Physicians have treated gynecological diseases from ancient times—and recorded their techniques and treatments. The oldest known medical text is the Kahun Gynecological Papyrus, which dates to about 1800 BCE. The papyrus, discovered in Egypt in 1889, discusses women's complaints, including fertility, pregnancy, and contraception. The works of the famous ancient Greek physician Hippocrates include gynecological treatises from the fifth to fourth centuries BCE.

Women physicians worked in Egypt as far back as circa 3150 to circa 2613 BCE. Merit-Ptah was the royal court's chief

This page from a medieval manuscript shows a woman preparing a simple herbal medicine.

physician circa 2700 BCE. In the Middle Ages women worked as herbalists, healers, and midwives, many treating women's illnesses. However, a woman was not allowed to practice as a physician or surgeon unless she was the spouse of a surgeon who died. In this case, the wife was allowed to take over her husband's practice in some European countries. Italy was at the forefront of educating women doctors. In twelfth-century Salerno, in Italy, the physician Trota of Salerno wrote several collections containing her medical practices, including one on women's health. Male writers of medieval medical texts from the Islamic Middle East mention women doctors who were employed to treat female patients because it was considered inappropriate for a man to touch a woman, especially her genitalia.

In America from the sixteenth to the early nineteenth centuries, the roles of women remained primarily those of nonphysician healers and midwives. In 1849, Elizabeth Blackwell became the first woman to graduate with a medical degree (from New York's Geneva Medical College). In 1853, she founded a clinic, which ultimately became the New York Infirmary for Women and Children. In 1868, she opened the Women's Medical College at the infirmary to train other female doctors. By the end of the nineteenth century, medical colleges for women had been established throughout the United States, Europe, and the Far East.

In the early twentieth century, Margaret Sanger worked as an obstetrical nurse in New York's poverty-stricken Lower East Side. Seeing the high rates of infant and maternal mortality and deaths from illegal abortions obtained by mothers who couldn't afford more children, she became a crusader for birth control. In 1916, Sanger opened the first birth control clinic, in Brooklyn, New York. In 1921, she established the American Birth Control League, which eventually became the Planned Parenthood Federation of American. The first birth control pill was invented in the 1960s.

Margaret Sanger was a crusader for birth control, which she believed would reduce deaths of poor women.

The women's liberation movement, which started in the late 1960s, led to increasing numbers of women pursuing careers. By the 1970s, a growing number of women were enrolling in medical schools and becoming physicians. The influx of female physicians altered many practices in gynecology so that it became more sensitive to the treatment and needs of women.

WOMEN'S HEALTH CARE SPECIALTIES

Women's health is not one homogeneous discipline. Experts in women's health care are employed in many different specialties.

THE OUTLOOK

According to the US Department of Labor's Bureau of Labor Statistics (BLS), all types of women's health care jobs are expected to grow significantly from 2014 to 2024. Employment for registered nurses (RNs) is expected to increase 16 percent by 2024, which is faster than the national average for all other occupations. The BLS also stated that registered nurses with at least a bachelor of science degree in nursing are expected to have the best job opportunities. Nurse anesthetist, nurse-midwife, and nurse practitioner opportunities are expected to grow 31 percent over this period. Demand for medical sonographers and cardiovascular technologists and technicians will grow 24 percent, while the demand for radiological technologists will increase 9 percent, and radiation therapist positions will increase 14 percent. The demand for nursing assistants will expand by 17 percent. Medical assistants will see an increase of 23 percent, and physicians and surgeons, including obstetricians and gynecologists, 14 percent.

Reasons for the rapid growth rate include expanded health care coverage, which has added an increasing number of patients to the system, and the aging population, because older people have more medical issues. Also, the improvement in the economy that has occurred in the decade since the economic crisis of 2008 has created greater employment across the economy. As a result, many adults in their twenties, who were living with their parents, are now moving into their own homes and starting families, which means more demands for women's health services. According to a study published in the *Journal of Women's Health*, there will likely be a modest 6 percent growth in women having babies between now and 2020 as the female population over age fourteen increases. However, because the number of women over the age of sixty-five will increase by 33 percent from 2010 to 2020, the demand for women's health services for older women is expected to increase much faster than that for basic obstetric services.

The following are some of the major areas in which one can work in women's health:

Obstetrics and gynecology. Obstetrics is the area of women's health that deals with pregnancy and childbirth. This discipline covers three time frames: the prenatal (before birth) period, delivering the baby, and the postnatal (after birth) care of the mother. In the prenatal period, the mother and the fetus are given regular checkups to make sure that the baby is developing normally and the mother remains healthy. During childbirth, the obstetrician makes sure that the baby is delivered safely and deals with any complications from the delivery. After giving birth, the mother and baby are monitored to make sure they recover appropriately.

Gynecology is a specialty that deals with the diagnosis and treatment of women's reproductive system disorders. Among the types of issues that a gynecologist deals with are cancer of the ovaries, uterus, or breasts; menstrual problems; and infections of the female reproduction system. Obstetrics and gynecology are often combined into one department.

Fertility and infertility treatment. When a couple has trouble conceiving a child, they may consult with a specialist who diagnoses issues that might be causing the problem and then administers one or more treatments in an attempt to help the couple achieve pregnancy. When a woman wishes to engage in family planning, she consults with a medical professional who can advise her of the pros and cons of various types of birth control. When a woman experiences an unwanted pregnancy, she may consult a physician at a facility that performs abortions.

Nutrition, weight management, and health and wellness. A variety of professionals assist women in staying healthy. Among these professionals are nutritionists, fitness trainers, and health educators. Women are educated about the appropriate way to manage their health, and a woman may continue to see the professional on a regular basis to work jointly on her program. Such training may take place in a hospital, medical center, or private facility.

Endocrinology and genetics. Endocrinology is the discipline that deals with issues related to hormones. Hormones are chemicals produced in the body that control bodily processes. When a person puts out too much or too little of a specific hormone, the bodily processes controlled by that hormone get out of whack, and the person experiences physical problems. Sometimes an imbalance in hormones affects a woman's overall health. At other times, such an imbalance may make it difficult for her to get pregnant. Conversely, sometimes pregnancy can cause a hormonal problem. Endocrinologists administer tests that identify hormonal problems and then prescribe treatments that alleviate the symptoms. Geneticists administer tests to identify whether parents and/or a fetus has the gene for an inherited disease.

Surgeons and rehabilitation experts. Gynecological surgeons deliver babies by cesarean section (an incision in the abdomen) when they can't be delivered naturally; they also repair damage to the reproductive organs. Oncological surgeons remove cancerous tumors. Other types of specialist surgeons operate on women with disorders that affect their area of specialty. For example, a cardiac surgeon operates on the heart and blood vessels. Rehabilitation nurses and technologists help women recover from surgery, strokes, and accidents. For instance, they supervise workouts to strengthen the heart after cardiac surgery or to strengthen the muscles after hip surgery.

Mental health and substance abuse specialists. Some mental health problems affect both genders equally, whereas others tend to affect women more than men, or vice versa. Women are more likely than men to suffer from clinical depression, for instance. Substance abuse counselors assist patients in dealing with alcohol and drug addiction. Psychopharmacologists (doctors who are expert in prescribing medication for psychological problems), psychiatrists, psychologists, and substance abuse counselors work in both inpatient and outpatient settings.

Gerontologists. Gerontologists specialize in the care of elderly patients. Often diseases and medications work differently in the elderly than in younger patients. Elderly patients often have multiple physical and/or mental health issues. Medications may be processed more slowly by elderly people. Therefore, they may build up in the patient's body, resulting in the symptoms of an overdose. A patient's mental state may affect his or her ability to comply with physicians' instructions. Therefore, a gerontologist may be called upon to take charge of elderly patients' care.

A gerontologist, trained to deal with the unique problems associated with aging, treats an elderly patient.

Home health care. One goal of modern health care is to get patients out of the hospital as quickly as possible and to provide as much care as possible in the home. Home health aides and visiting nurses provide in-home care for patients who are injured, ill, or recovering from surgery. In addition, home health aides provide services to elderly people who need assistance with daily activities.

SETTINGS FOR WOMEN'S HEALTH CARE

Women's health care is administered in a variety of settings. Therefore, when considering a career, you not only have to decide what type of job would suit you but also what type of environment you would like to work in. The following are some settings in which women's health care takes place:

Physicians' offices. The doctor may be part of a group practice with other doctors or have a standalone office (private practice).

Clinics. There are a variety of specialty clinics that offer women's health care services, including fertility clinics, family planning clinics, community health care clinics, and mental health and substance abuse treatment centers.

Hospitals. In addition to general hospitals, women's health care is offered at maternity, rehabilitation, and mental hospitals.

Public health agencies. These agencies perform studies of social and environmental factors that affect women's health and enact policies designed to keep women healthy.

Education and research facilities. Researchers at universities and medical facilities study diseases and attempt to develop new and better ways to treat them. Educators at schools train professionals to treat disorders and disease.

A physician in a private practice treats women patients throughout the various phases of their life and advises them on ways to stay healthy.

Senior care residences and nursing homes. Professionals at nursing homes and senior residences provide both health and support services to people who are elderly and people who are recuperating from injury or surgery.

Hospices. Professionals who work in hospices provide supportive care to people who have terminal diseases.

chapter 2

PREPARING FOR A WOMEN'S HEALTH CAREER

Education for careers in women's health care ranges from on-the-job training, to programs that take several months, to two-year associate's degree programs, to jobs requiring a college and medical school degree. One can start laying the foundation for a career in women's health while still in high school.

HIGH SCHOOL PREPARATION

If you are interested in pursuing a career in women's health care, take as many science courses as possible. In particular, chemistry and biology courses will help you understand course material in on-the-job and higher education programs. Physics courses are extremely useful if you are interested in a technical area such as medical imaging or radiology. Many cities and towns have vocational high schools, which offer practical career courses. If you are interested in a nursing career, it's worth checking to see if there is a vocational program for becoming a medical, nursing, or laboratory assistant.

It is expected that medical professionals at all levels will be adept at dealing sensitively and supportively with patients.

Taking science courses such as biology and chemistry in high school is an excellent way to prepare for a career in women's health.

Courses in the humanities, such as history, can help you to better understand other people's backgrounds and cultural concerns. Learning at least one other language can help you better communicate with patients and will be an asset when applying for a job. Which language is most beneficial will depend on the populations of the area in which you live or would like to practice. Among the most common are Spanish, Russian, Arabic, Chinese, and French.

Computer technology plays a role in all aspects of a health care career, so learning about it will help on the job. Take advantage of a high school's computer science courses to get a leg up on others entering the health care field.

It is also necessary to learn to communicate well with colleagues and staff members, both in writing and verbally. Medical staff members spend a great deal of time talking with physicians, other staff members, and patients, and documenting information in written form. Learning the rules of English grammar and composition and how to communicate ideas clearly can help you provide information accurately and avoid any misunderstandings. Medical professionals constantly use computers—to enter and transmit patient data, check patients' histories, evaluate symptoms, and write reports. Many use tablets as they carry out their work around the facility. So, if your school offers computer training, take it. Computer technology is constantly changing—the better you understand the principles, the easier you'll find it to make the transition to new programs and technologies. For the same reason, if your school offers a typing or keyboarding course, take it; it will speed up your data entry.

GAINING EXPERIENCE WHILE IN SCHOOL

If you are seeking an entry-level job in women's health care or trying to gain entry to a training program directly out of high school, you will be competing against many other candidates. One way to make yourself stand out is to obtain some experience while you are still in high school. For example, volunteer at a hospital, health clinic, or nursing home. In some cases, it may be possible to obtain part-time or summer employment at a medical facility. Working in such an environment gives you the chance to observe what medical staff do daily. This knowledge can help you decide if the health care field is right for you, and the experience provides the opportunity to understand what skills you'll need to succeed. Furthermore, working with medical staff and patients helps you to develop the interpersonal skills necessary to work successfully in a medical environment. Beyond this, working with medical professionals provides you with contacts who may be willing to supply you with recommendations when you apply for a job or may be able to assist you with job hunting.

You can get information on part-time and volunteer opportunities by contacting the human resources department of local hospitals, clinics, and nursing homes. Often major hospitals have a volunteer coordinator, who manages volunteers.

EDUCATION FOR HOSPITAL AND HEALTH CARE CAREERS

Requirements for specific jobs vary widely and are described later under each job. The following are some general guidelines. Courses for health care jobs are offered by hospitals, technical and vocational schools, community colleges, specialized schools such as colleges of nursing, and conventional colleges. In some cases, it is possible to complete coursework online as well. If you take the online approach to obtaining a two-year associate's degree, it is a good idea to check the US Department of Education's online database of accredited schools (http://ope.ed.gov/accreditation/Search .aspx) to make sure that the school is accredited. In some cases, passing a certification test is the objective. In this case, where you take a course is not as important as learning the material itself and passing the test.

Nursing students undergo training to learn procedures such as how to prepare a medication and insert a needle or an intravenous drip feed into a patient's arm.

CERTIFICATION AND LICENSING

Many jobs in women's health care require certification or licensing. Certification is provided by industry organizations, such as the American Midwifery Certification Board, whereas licensing is provided by individual states. In both cases, applicants must meet the educational requirements and take a test demonstrating that they have mastered the subject matter in their field. Certifications and licensing requirements for specific jobs are described later under specific jobs. Often, books and online courses are available to help people practice for the tests. Some of these materials are offered by industry organizations, and others are created by third parties.

chapter 3

NURSES IN WOMEN'S HEALTH CARE

Many different types of nurses work in women's health care. Nurses provide care to patients in hospitals according to the orders of a physician. They administer medication, draw blood, check vital signs (pulse, temperature, and blood pressure), and ensure that patients' needs are met while they are in the hospital.

CERTIFIED NURSING ASSISTANTS

A certified nursing assistant (CNA) works under the supervision of a registered nurse to assist patients or clients. They help patients with their physical needs, such as eating, washing, and dressing. CNAs work in hospitals, long-term-care facilities, and hospices. In long-term-care facilities, they often handle most of the patient-related daily activities. Hospitals, technical schools, vocational schools, and home health agencies offer training programs for CNAs. Most states require a high school diploma or GED, but there are a few that allow sixteen-year-olds with at least eight years of schooling to apply without one. You need to complete a course consisting of 75 to 140 hours (two to eight weeks) of training. CNAs must be certified. This stipulation is true of all medical facilities in all states that accept patients under the Medicare and/or Medicaid

A certified nursing assistant helps an elderly patient in a nursing home, making it easier for the patient to accomplish daily living tasks.

programs. The Medicare and/or Medicaid programs' guidelines require CNAs working at these facilities to undergo a competency evaluation within four months of their being hired. To meet the certification requirements, CNAs must take a written competency exam such as the National Nurse's Aide Assessment Program exam that is administered by the National Council on State Boards of Nursing.

LICENSED PRACTICAL NURSE

Licensed practical nurses (LPNs), who sometimes are called licensed vocational nurses (LVNs), care for patients who are disabled, ill, or injured. Licensed visiting nurses are a type of licensed practical nurse employed by home health care agencies. Licensed visiting nurses perform their tasks in a patient's home, whereas other LPNs work in medical facilities. The tasks they perform, however, are similar. They work under the direction of registered nurses. They assist patients with tasks such as washing, eating, and dressing. Unlike CNAs, they also take patients' vital signs and change dressings on wounds. They help physicians during patient exams, record patient information, and perform administrative work. To become an LPN, a person takes a twelve- to eighteen-month training program. The program includes coursework in anatomy and physiology, first aid, various types of nursing procedures, and medication administration, among other topics. It also requires practical training in a hospital setting. Technical schools, community colleges, and hospitals provide LPN training programs. Short training programs provide graduates with a certificate, whereas longer programs gain them a diploma. Following completion of the training program, students must pass a licensing test from the state licensing board in the state where they will practice.

REGISTERED NURSES

Registered nurses (RNs) have completed either a two- or four-year degree program at the college level. After obtaining a degree, registered nurses must pass the National Council Licensure Examination–Registered Nurse licensing test offered by the National Council of State Boards of Nursing and the state board of nursing in the state where they wish to practice. However, generally hospitals prefer those applying for most registered nurse positions to have a four-year bachelor's degree in nursing. Registered nurses with associate's degrees are most likely to be employed in lower-level nursing positions.

RNs work in all types of medical facilities that offer women's health services. They take patients' vital signs and monitor and record their progress under the direction of physicians. They operate medical equipment and perform diagnostic tests. They administer treatment and medications prescribed by physicians. They assist in treating patients with medical emergencies. They supervise LPNs and CNAs. RNs educate both patients

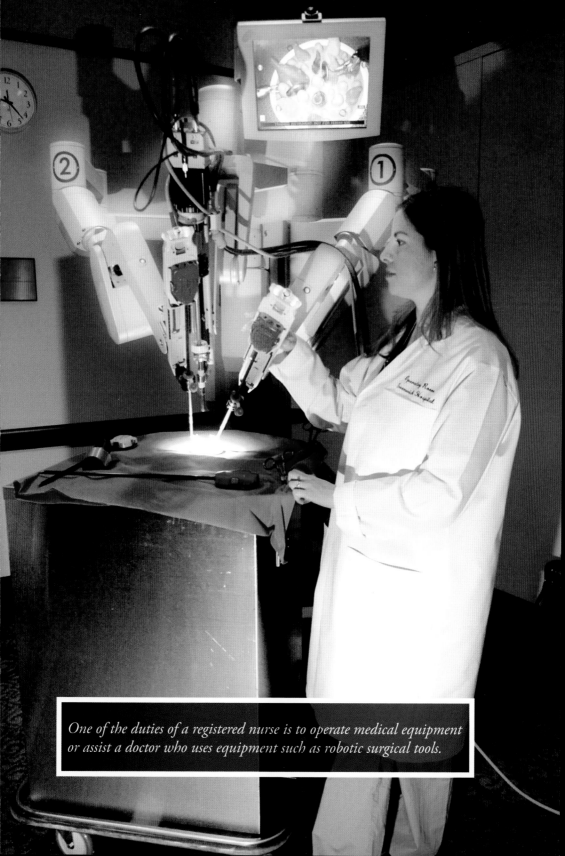

One of the duties of a registered nurse is to operate medical equipment or assist a doctor who uses equipment such as robotic surgical tools.

and their families about the patients' conditions and the treatments to be carried out in the facility and at home.

Nurses often spend a great deal of time standing and walking. They also have to lift and move patients and equipment, which puts strain on their backs. Further, it's important for nurses to follow strict guidelines for working in an environment where they come in contact with infectious diseases.

In hospitals, clinics, and rehabilitation and residential facilities, nurses are on-site around the clock, so the workday is divided into several shifts, including a nightshift. Nurses might have to work on weekends and holidays. Some nurses may be on call, which means that they may have to come in to work if there is a situation that requires more staff.

ASSISTANCE FOR TRAINING

Assistance in paying for health care training and education is available from various sources. It's common for technical schools and colleges to have a financial aid department, which helps students apply for financial aid. Student loans are available from banks. The government controls the interest rates that banks can charge, but the loans must be repaid, except in cases when the graduate takes certain nonprofit or government service jobs.

Low-income students can apply for a US Federal Supplemental Education Opportunity Grant (see the website https://www2 .ed.gov/programs/fseog). This program provides funds to low-income students for education. Some schools offer work-study programs. In this case, the student works part-time for the school for pay. Low-income students who want to study nursing are also eligible for grants from the Health Resources and Services Administration (HRSA), which is part of the US Department of

Health and Human Services. Funds for this program are given to schools, which, in turn, choose recipients. For more information, check the HRSA website (https://www.hrsa.gov/loanscholarships /scholarships/disadvantaged.html) or the school's financial aid office. In addition, some states offer grants for nursing students. To find out if your state offers grants, check with the state department of public health. Under the GI Bill, veterans and the children of veterans are eligible for educational assistance. Children of veterans can check with the Veterans Administration (http://www.benefits .va.gov/gibill/) to see what educational financing programs they might be able to access. Finally, if you get any job at a hospital, even if it is not related to nursing, you may be eligible to take training offered by the hospital free of charge.

SPECIALTY NURSES

Nurses can work in an area of practice that requires specialized expertise. Specialty nurses undergo advanced education, training, and certification. The following list describes some types of specialty nursing encountered in women's health care:

Nurse anesthetist. Nurse anesthetists are RNs who administer anesthesia to patients during surgery. Prior to surgery, they evaluate patients to establish the best and safest method of anesthesia for them. They monitor the patient during surgery to make sure the correct amount of anesthesia is administered and after surgery to make sure the patient comes out of anesthesia appropriately.

Critical care nurse. Critical care nurses work in intensive care, critical care, and cardiac units. They must carry out complex treatments and provide continuous supervision of patients who are extremely ill, have life-threatening injuries, or are recovering from surgeries on organs such as the

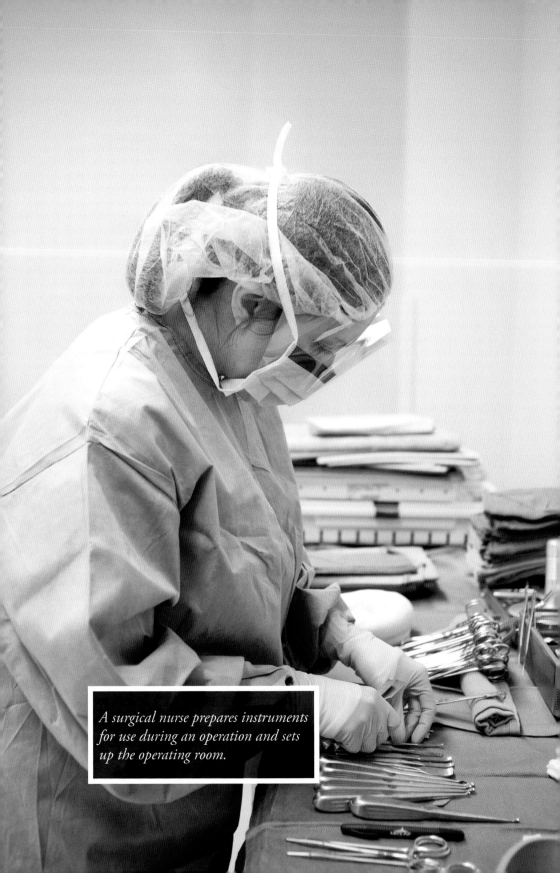

A surgical nurse prepares instruments for use during an operation and sets up the operating room.

heart, in which complications could result in death. Critical care nursing is a high-intensity and high-stress job.

Labor and delivery nurse. Labor and delivery nurses care for women who are having babies. They assist the obstetrician during surgery and monitor the mother and baby during the delivery process. They also care for the newborn immediately after it is born.

Surgical nurse. Surgical nurses work in operating rooms. They prepare the operating room for the surgery, set out the tools, and make sure the area where the surgery will take place is sterile. They assist the members of the surgical team with dressing in sterile clothing, gloves, and masks. During the surgery, they pass instruments to the surgeon. When the surgery is complete, they clear away tools and prepare the patient to be moved to the recovery room. RN first assistants are surgical nurses with more advanced training. They monitor the patient's vital signs prior to, during, and after surgery, and they let the physician know if a problem arises. Surgical nurses work in both inpatient and day-surgery units.

Neonatal critical care nurses. Neonatal intensive care unit registered nurses (NICU RNs) work in critical care units especially for babies. They provide care to babies who are premature, sick, or addicted because their mothers were addicts. NICU RNs must provide round-the-clock care to babies. They perform both routine care, such as feeding and bathing babies, and specialized care, working with equipment such as incubators, which keep babies warm, and ventilators, which help them breathe. They also provide support to parents and educate them about how to care for their baby at home. Like working in adult critical care, being an NICU RN is a high-intensity and high-stress job.

chapter 4

WOMEN'S DOCTORS

There are a number of specialty areas of women's health care in which physicians practice. The education required to become a doctor is covered here, followed by a look at specific women's health specialties.

BECOMING A DOCTOR

To become a physician, the first step is to obtain a four-year college degree. One does not have to major in science. However, medical schools require applicants to have taken courses in biology, chemistry, and statistics. After graduating, one must attend medical school. Medical school lasts four years. Students spend the first two years taking courses about the human body, biochemistry, and diseases and disorders, among other subjects. In the second two years, medical students rotate through different hospital departments. They work on basic medical tasks under the direction of physicians and residents (student doctors). Upon graduating they are doctors. Doctors are licensed by the state medical boards in the state where they practice. Applicants must meet educational and training requirements and pass a written and an oral exam.

However, to meet the requirements to practice in a specialty, such as obstetrics-gynecology, and have the right to work at a hospital, doctors must serve a residency in the specialty they are interested in. The lengths of residencies

Student doctors, called residents, go on rounds, seeing patients with a physician who teaches them about treating women's ailments.

vary by specialty. An obstetrics-gynecology residency typically lasts four years. Residents work as doctors under the supervision of a fully qualified physician. Upon completing a residency, a doctor can become certified in the specialty by passing a test that is administered by the medical board for that specialty, such as the American Board of Medical Specialties or the American Board of Obstetrics and Gynecology. Hospitals around the country also offer fellowships for additional training for those interested in pursuing a particular subspecialty in women's health, such as reproductive endocrinology and fertility, female pelvic medicine

PHYSICIAN ASSISTANTS AND NURSE PRACTITIONERS

Physician assistants and nurse practitioners provide basic medical diagnosis and treatment of patients. They perform a variety of medical procedures under the supervision of a physician. Physician assistants obtain a bachelor's degree and then go on to complete a two-year master's physician assistant program. Nurse-practitioners are registered nurses with a least a bachelor's degree, who then go on to obtain a master's degree or PhD in nursing and receive an advanced practice registered nurse license. Both physician assistant and nurse practitioner programs include classroom and clinical instruction in areas including anatomy, physiology, pathology (disease), clinical medicine, medical laws and ethics, and pharmacology. In practice physician assistants and nurse practitioners interview and examine patients, order tests, give injections and vaccinations, prescribe medication, suture wounds, and educate patients about health and wellness.

and reconstructive surgery, maternal-fetal medicine, or gynecologic oncology (cancer treatment). Fellows practice in the subspecialty and conduct research. Even after becoming a fully qualified doctor, physicians must take a certain number of continuing education courses every year to remain certified.

WOMEN'S HEALTH SPECIALTIES

The following are some types of physicians who practice in the women's health field:

Obstetrician-gynecologists (OBGYNs). OBGYNs diagnose and treat diseases of the female reproductive system. They assist patients with issues that relate to family planning, the menstrual cycle, infertility, pregnancy, and childbirth. They administer tests to identify problems with women's reproductive organs. They also deliver babies. When a woman is unable to deliver a baby naturally, the obstetrician might have to perform a type of surgery called a cesarean section. This surgery involves making an incision in the woman's abdomen and removing the baby. OBGYNs usually spend some time working in an office and some time in a hospital. Because there is no way to determine when a baby will be born or an

A gynecological oncologist examines a mammogram (breast X-ray) to evaluate a female patient's cancer.

emergency will arise, their working hours can be irregular and unpredictable.

Gynecological oncologists. Gynecologic oncologists diagnose and treat cancer of the female reproductive system, including cancer of the breast, cervix, ovaries, and uterus. They order tests such as mammograms and ultrasound scans, and they perform diagnostic procedures such as biopsies (removal of a small amount of tissue) to identify cancer. They draw up plans that include treatments such as radiation therapy and chemotherapy. Gynecological oncologist surgeons remove cancer from the body surgically. Aside from their medical responsibilities, they educate patients and their families on the type of cancer, likely progression, and treatment options.

Endocrinologists. Endocrinology is the study and treatment of conditions related to human hormones. Hormones are chemicals produced by organs called glands. They travel through the bloodstream to various organs and regulate bodily functions and behavior. An example of a hormonal disorder is diabetes, in which there is too much sugar in the blood because of a lack of the hormone insulin. Most endocrine disorders are diseases that require lifelong care. Endocrinologists order blood tests to diagnose diseases and prescribe medications to control hormone levels. They must educate patients about proper behavior and diet to assist in controlling their disease.

Geneticists. Clinical geneticists evaluate and care for patients with genetic diseases. They screen patients for conditions and diseases that are inherited or result from altered DNA. To be a clinical geneticist one must have a bachelor's degree in a biology or physical science field, become a doctor, and then complete six years of

A geneticist examines a DNA test, checking for results that would indicate that the patient carries the genes for an inherited disease.

residency and training to earn certification from the American Board of Medical Genetics. Among the inherited diseases a clinical geneticist deals with are Alzheimer's disease, cystic fibrosis, hemophilia, Tay-Sachs disease, and sickle-cell disease, as well as some types of cancer. Clinical geneticists are often consulted by couples who are thinking of having children and have a family history of a genetic disease. In addition to seeing patients, some clinical geneticists supervise laboratory technicians who perform the DNA analysis tests.

chapter 5

DELIVERING BABIES

The most central career in women's health is that of midwife. Midwives deliver babies. Midwives today are formally trained and licensed. Most midwives who work in hospitals and clinics are nurse-midwives.

A BRIEF HISTORY OF MIDWIFERY

From ancient times through the eighteenth century, the care of pregnant women and delivering of babies were considered inappropriate duties for male physicians, and these functions were performed instead by midwives. Most births took place at home. Historically, midwives were mothers themselves who attended the births of neighbors or family members. Although they didn't have a formal education, some midwives gained extensive knowledge of herbal remedies and treated women's other medical problems as well. Older married or widowed women often adopted midwifery as an occupation because it provided them with income in the form of money or goods. Physicians and surgeons were called only when there was a serious complication.

In the early nineteenth century, "lying-in" hospitals began to be established, and physicians began to take control of the birthing process. However, a stigma remained

A print from the sixteenth century depicts a midwife as she delivers a baby in a woman's home with the assistance of a female relative of the patient.

attached to men who were involved in obstetrics, on the grounds that delivering babies—indeed having anything to do with children—was unmanly. In addition, because the nature of germs wasn't understood, doctors didn't wash their hands between deliveries, often transferring germs from one patient to the next, resulting in very high levels of infection and maternal death. The death rate due to "childbed fever" was considerably lower among women who had babies at home. Because of these issues, midwives continued to deliver most babies.

By the late nineteenth century, most European countries were monitoring the training of midwives and requiring them to be certified. In the 1880s, Dr. Ignaz Semmelweis observed that washing one's hands with antiseptic between deliveries reduced the infection rate, and he promoted this practice. By the end of the nineteenth century, major advancements in anesthesia and the development of the cesarean section made having a baby in a hospital more desirable. At the same time, advances in procedures to treat conditions concerning the female reproductive system led to the creation of gynecology as a specialty. The move to having babies at hospitals meant that obstetricians replaced midwives as the professional involved in the birth process. Nonetheless, many women continued to have babies at home attended by midwives in the first half of the twentieth century. After World War II, having a baby at a hospital attended by an obstetrician became the modern norm, with 88 percent of births occurring in hospitals by the 1950s, according to an article by Neal Dewitt in the journal *Birth*.

In the 1960s and 1970s, women began to demand more control over their own bodies. Many chose to give birth naturally at home rather than be drugged with anesthesia and have the process controlled by a doctor, usually a man at that time.

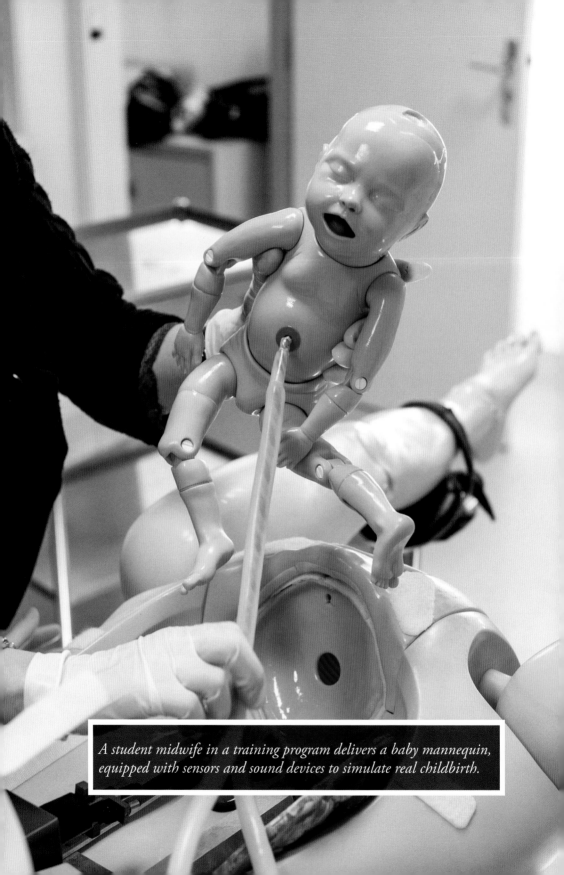

A student midwife in a training program delivers a baby mannequin, equipped with sensors and sound devices to simulate real childbirth.

The demand for midwives began to increase again. In the late twentieth century, hospitals, wanting to continue to attract patients, installed birth centers offering a greater variety of options for giving birth and started training programs for nurse-midwives.

WHAT A MIDWIFE DOES

Certified nurse-midwives (CNMs), certified midwives (CMs), and certified professional midwives (CPMs) assist women during pregnancy, when delivering a baby, and after the birth. CMs and CPMs undergo training and must pass a certification exam but do not have nursing training. Nurse-midwives are registered nurses who also have midwife training. All certified midwives and nurse-midwives teach women techniques to prepare for the birth process, deliver the baby, and provide training in the care of the newborn. CPMs are specifically trained in home delivery of babies. Nurse-midwives, because of their more extensive medical training, work closely with obstetricians and gynecologists to care for women with both short-term and chronic illnesses, in addition to assisting in the birth process. Nurse-midwives are different from obstetric nurses, who perform standard nursing functions but do not deliver babies. CNMs examine patients, take medical histories, perform diagnostics, or order tests to be carried out by technologists. Some states allow CNMs to prescribe medications.

All types of midwives work with women of various ages, from teens to those entering menopause. They work with women of all cultures and ethnic backgrounds. They must be sensitive, caring, patient, and tolerant of cultural differences. Because they work with nurses, technologists, and physicians as part of a team, they must work well with others and communicate clearly.

Midwives work as team members with other health care professionals and must learn to work with women of various ethnic and cultural backgrounds, remaining sensitive to cultural differences.

TRAINING AND CERTIFICATION

To become a certified nurse-midwife, one must be a licensed registered nurse with a bachelor's degree in nursing. RNs with an associate's degree can usually take a one- to two-year program that allows them to convert the associate's degree to a bachelor's degree in nursing. CNMs complete an accredited master of science program with a concentration in midwifery. Certified midwives must have a background in a

MIDWIFE CERTIFICATION EXAM

The American Midwifery Certification Board (AMCB) administers certified nurse-midwife and certified midwife exams. The North American Registry of Midwives offers the Certified Professional Midwife certification. Midwifery certification exams are designed to test applicants' knowledge and judgment. The exams test their knowledge of both performing normal births and responding to deviations from normal. The tests cover antepartum (before birth), birth, and postpartum (after birth) knowledge. The AMCB exam also covers women's health/primary care, gynecology, contraception, and newborn care. The following is an example of a typical question from the AMCB practice exam:

1. A client is in the second stage of labor and has been pushing for almost an hour. Which of the following interventions is the most appropriate for the client at this stage?

A. Offer clear fluids in between contractions.
B. Encourage ambulation.
C. Instruct the client to push with each contraction.
D. Encourage frequent changes in position.

Answer: C

(Source for sample exam question: "Certified Professional Midwife Exam Prep." Practice Quiz. Retrieved March 22, 2017. https://www.practicequiz.com/question/12388.)

health-related field other than nursing and must graduate from an accredited midwifery education program. CMs and CNMs take the same certification exam from ACMB, but

Becoming a certified midwife requires taking an accredited midwife training course, guaranteeing that the midwife has up-to-date skills.

they receive different professional designations. The Certified Professional Midwife (CPM) certification, issued by the North American Registry of Midwives, is available in twenty-six states. CPM candidates obtain the required education by serving an apprenticeship, attending an accredited midwife degree program, or submitting proof that they have the necessary professional experience. Certified midwives and nurse-midwives must complete recertification every three to five years, depending on their certification, to ensure that their skills stay current.

chapter 6

WOMEN'S HEALTH TECHNICAL AND SUPPORT CAREERS

Various types of nonmedical personnel are required as part of the women's health care team. These people perform tests; train, counsel, and care for patients; and study and advocate for ways to improve women's health.

PATIENT ASSISTANCE JOBS

Patient assistance jobs involve helping a patient make arrangements for care or providing such care. The most common patient assistance jobs include the following:

Social service aide. Social service aides help hospital patients make arrangements for home health care and for community and government services, such as Medicare or Medicaid. They also arrange admission and transfer of hospital patients, following hospital treatment, to "step-down" facilities such as nursing homes, rehabilitative facilities, or hospices. They may assist the hospital social worker with other tasks. This job usually requires only a high school diploma. Those in this position may later choose to pursue additional education to obtain a bachelor's degree to become a social worker.

A social services aide assists a patient in arranging for support and rehabilitation services after she leaves the hospital.

Personal care aide. Personal care aides provide assistance with daily living tasks such as bathing, eating, and dressing. They may cook food, perform house-cleaning activities, and run errands. They may also drive patients to places such as the doctor's office. In addition to providing services during scheduled visits, some home health care companies provide "sitter" services. A personal care aide may be asked to stay with a person for several hours or even a whole day while the person's caregiver is away. Personal care aides may work for a home health care company on a full-time or part-time basis, so this job provides flexibility. This job does not require any special education. A pleasant personality, patience, and reliability are key factors in succeeding in this position.

Certified home health aide. Certified home health aides visit patients in their homes. They set up equipment and train patients and caretakers on how to use it. They take patients' vital signs, record information about their symptoms, administer medication, and report any issues with a patient's mental, physical, or emotional condition to the nurse in charge of the patient's case. They may also assist patients with personal care tasks.

Certified home health aides must complete a certified nursing assistant or home health aide course. These courses take place over several weeks and are available at technical schools, hospitals, and community colleges. Following completion of the course, students must pass a competency exam to demonstrate they have mastered the material. One such exam is the National Nurse's Aide Assessment Program exam administered by the National Council on State Boards of Nursing.

TECHNOLOGISTS

Technologists perform tests ordered by physicians, physician assistants, and nurse-midwives. They work with various types of electronic medical equipment. Some technologists who commonly perform tests in women's health care are the following:

Cardiovascular technologist. Cardiovascular technologists use an electrocardiogram (EKG) machine to test heart function. They use Holter monitors (portable EKG machines worn by patients), stress-testing equipment, echocardiographs (which use sound waves to provide images of the

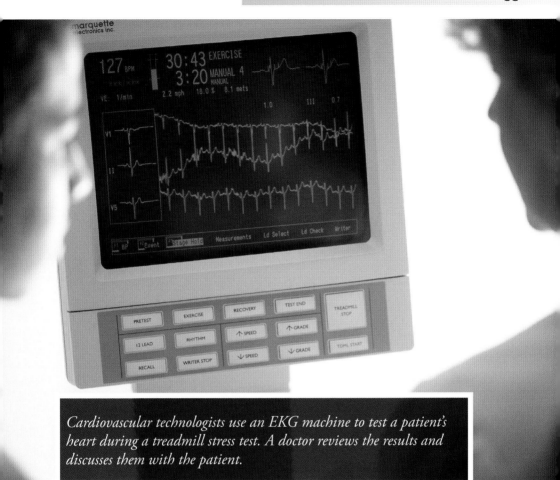

Cardiovascular technologists use an EKG machine to test a patient's heart during a treadmill stress test. A doctor reviews the results and discusses them with the patient.

heart), and cardiac Doppler units, which use sound waves to measure the output of blood from the heart. Most cardiovascular technologists complete a two-year program and receive an associate's degree. They may specialize in the operation of particular types of cardiovascular testing equipment. After completing training, they are eligible for certification.

Electroencephalogram technologist. Electroencephalogram (ECG) technologists operate a machine that analyzes brain waves to see if brain activity is normal or abnormal. High school graduates can either undergo a one-year on-the-job training program or take a one- or two-year training program at a community college, technical school, or college.

Radiological technologist/radiation therapy technologist. Radiological technologists use X-ray machines to perform mammograms to see if women have breast cancer. Radiation therapy technologists operate equipment that is used to administer radiation treatments to cancer patients. One can qualify for these positions by taking a one- or two-year certificate program or a two-year associate's degree program. Those who wish to move on to a supervisory position can pursue additional education and obtain a bachelor's degree.

Sonographer. Sonographers operate ultrasound equipment, which uses sound waves to create images of unborn babies and to identify abnormalities in women's bodies. Sonographers position the patient, apply gel to the patient's skin, and run a handheld device over the area being scanned, adjusting the equipment to obtain a clear image. Sonographers complete a two-year associate's degree program. Sonographers can take an exam offered by the Society of Medical Diagnostic Sonographers to become certified.

LAB TECHNICIANS AND LAB ASSISTANTS

Lab technicians and assistants prepare samples of blood, tissue, and other bodily substances. They run tests for pregnancy and diseases experienced by women. Clinical laboratory technicians, also called clinical laboratory assistants, perform the simpler tests, such as blood tests. In addition, they prepare tissue samples for examination and perform other routine laboratory procedures. Clinical laboratory technologists supervise clinical laboratory assistants and perform more advanced tests. A clinical laboratory technician requires a two-year associate's degree. Clinical laboratory clinicians can obtain

A lab technician tests samples using automated equipment, such as this centrifuge, which is used to process blood samples.

certification by a variety of organizations, including the American Society of Clinical Pathology Board of Certification and the National Accrediting Agency for Clinical Laboratory Sciences, among others. Clinical laboratory technologists obtain a bachelor's degree and certification.

MEDICAL ASSISTANT

Medical assistants help women's doctors in private and hospital-based offices. They perform a combination of clerical and medical work. They set up exam rooms; record patients' height, weight, pulse, and temperature; and assist doctors during procedures. They also schedule appointments, keep records, code medical records for billing purposes, generate paperwork for prescriptions and lab tests, and order and stock supplies. Community colleges, general colleges and universities, and technical schools offer one-year certificate and two-year associate's degree programs. The American Association of Medical Assistants and the American Medical Technologists provide certification.

BIRTH TRAINER/DOULA

Birth trainers prepare women and their partners to participate optimally in the birth of their child. Doulas provide training and emotional support during pregnancy, birth, and the post-birth period. They provide women with information to help them make decisions about where and in what manner they want to give birth. Doulas also educate women on the nonmedical aspects of labor, such as breathing, positions and movement, and other techniques to make giving birth less stressful. After birth, they teach women about newborn care and breastfeeding. This occupation is a nonmedical position. If doulas observe a possible medical issue, they report it to a medical professional for assessment. Doulas take a training course either in person or online, which takes about twelve weeks. Courses and certification are offered by a variety of organizations such as the Childbirth and Postpartum Professional Association (CAPPA) and the International Doula Institute. Doulas may work at clinics or hospitals or be employed by a health care agency, which sends them to assist women at partner hospitals or at home.

COUNSELORS

Mental health, substance abuse, and domestic violence counselors help women work through and recover from

WOMEN'S HEALTH ADVOCACY

Women's health advocates work in settings such as family-planning and community clinics and in women's shelters. They assist women with abuse and family-planning issues and promote women's well-being and safety. In residential facilities, such as women's shelters, advocates are responsible for providing a safe living environment for residents. They assist women with obtaining counseling, legal representation, and support, and with job hunting, as necessary. They assess each woman's needs and arrange appropriate services, including maternal and child health and nutrition, parenting, child development, financial literacy education, and employment skills training. Women's health advocates usually have at least a bachelor's degree in a social service area such as social work or psychology. Speaking a second language common in the area where one is seeking work is helpful. The work can be rewarding but also often can be stressful.

problems in these areas. Counselors must have at least a bachelor's degree in psychology or social work, and most have a master's degree. Some have a PhD. A psychiatrist is a medical doctor with a specialty in psychology. Psychiatrists can prescribe medication in addition to providing counseling. Non-MD counselors can receive certification from organizations such as the National Board for Certified Counselors (NBCC) or the Commission on Rehabilitation Counselor Certification (CRCC). All counselors must be licensed by the state in which they practice. Licensing requires that the applicant have the required level of education and training and pass a licensing exam. Counselors typically give guidance to clients one-on-one or in groups. They may also field crisis hotline calls, train and supervise students and volunteers, and give workshops. Often they are called upon to participate in community outreach, making presentations to community agencies and the public. They may work with representatives of other organizations.

PUBLIC HEALTH JOBS

Public health issues often disproportionately affect women and their children. Public health nurse and advocate jobs are frequently filled by nurses who have experience dealing with women's health. Community health nurses visit women who are deemed to be at risk because of the environment in which they live. Frequently they have to deal with issues of domestic abuse, poverty, or substance abuse. They may be involved in training new parents in proper childcare.

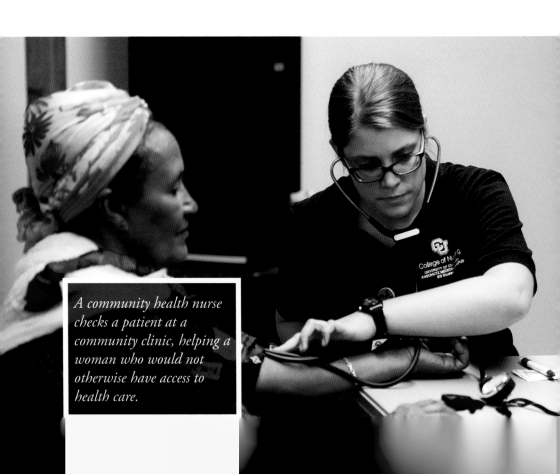

A community health nurse checks a patient at a community clinic, helping a woman who would not otherwise have access to health care.

Public health nurses also investigate reports of communicable diseases, conducting follow-up visits as necessary, and write reports. They may organize and attend immunization clinics. They also provide a wide range of nursing services, including vaccinating and testing first responders such as police and firefighters.

Epidemiologists conduct research to better understand the frequency and causes of diseases or problems such as domestic violence or inadequate nutrition. Such jobs involve preparing surveys, designing research plans, and conducting in-person and database research.

Jobs in public health research exist at all levels from intern to PhD. The jobs generally require at least a bachelor's degree in public health, nursing, biology, or a social science. Higher-level jobs require an advanced degree.

chapter 7

LANDING A JOB AND ADVANCEMENT

Once you have completed training and decided where to work, it is time to search for a job. This section describes the steps that are involved in obtaining a position.

LOCATING POTENTIAL JOBS

Because there is a shortage of qualified health care workers in many locations, finding a job in this field may be easier than in other professions. The most obvious way to locate potential work is through online job-hunting sites such as Monster.com, CareerBuilder.com, and the like. There are various other ways to locate potential jobs as well.

If you take a course as part of the preparation for a health care career, the school may offer job placement resources. Technical schools and colleges usually have a job placement office that helps students find jobs. This office may also provide assistance with job-hunting skills and preparing résumés.

There is a high turnover in health care support jobs, and the increasing demand for services creates a continuous need for additional staff. Therefore, hospitals and home health care agencies frequently develop openings for personnel. Many institutions accept applications for positions on-site. It is possible to obtain a list of hospitals, clinics, residential facilities, and home health

Many schools that offer health care training courses provide assistance with placement services or assistance with job hunting for students and graduates.

care agencies in your area from the online Yellow Pages or a general online search by type of facility and your city or state. You can call the human resources department at these companies and see if positions are available. Some facilities, especially hospitals and medical centers, have an on-site placement office, which you can visit in person.

Another source of jobs is temporary help agencies. There are companies that specialize in supplying personnel to medical facilities on an as-needed basis. Check for employment agencies that specialize in health care.

Many companies today advertise job openings on their own websites as well as on general job-listing sites. So check out the

"Careers" or "Jobs" section of facilities in your area. In addition, try the website of the professional organization that covers your job area. Often professional organizations maintain online lists of job openings for members. Some professional organizations also provide information on internship positions for students in their profession. Internships are unpaid positions that give students a chance to learn about a job while still in school. Internships are sometimes listed on online job-hunting sites as well. Do a search for one in your area of interest: for example, "public health internship."

PREPARING YOUR RÉSUMÉ

When applying for a job, it is necessary to supply potential employers with a résumé. A résumé is a document that lists one's skills, experience, and training. The purpose of the résumé is to convince the company to give the applicant an interview. Therefore, you should focus on the skills that apply specifically to the jobs being applied for.

Use a simple, easy-to-follow format. Start with personal information such as name, address, phone number, and email address. Then, list any jobs you've had, with the most recent first. Include part-time and summer jobs and volunteer jobs you have performed at health care facilities or nursing homes.

Next, list your education. Include any certificate or degree courses you have taken, and list any certifications and licenses you have obtained. If you apply for a job directly out of high school, without completing a formal training program, you will need to demonstrate to potential employers that you can handle the job despite not having much work experience. List relevant courses that you have taken in high school, such as biology, chemistry, physics, computer courses, and any vocational courses that provided medical, technical, or clerical skills.

Maya Rodriguez
123 Winton Road
Boston, MA
Home Phone: (555) 123-4567
Cell Phone: (555) 777-7777
Email: MayaRodriquez@none.com

OBJECTIVE:
A certified nursing assistant position in women's health.

PROFESSIONAL EXPERIENCE
ABC Hospice, 123 Squabb Street, Boston, MA, 2017–Present
Nursing Aide Intern
• Maintain the comfort of patients by providing personal care under the supervision of RN
• Support patients and help them maintain their independence
• Assist RN by obtaining samples, weights, and vital signs of patients
• Oversee patients' intake of medication
• Observe status of patients and report changes and needs for medication to the RN and physicians
• Create a healthy, safe environment for patients by keeping areas clean and neat

Friendly Women's Birthing Center, 343 Divisible Street, Boston, MA, 2015-2016
Volunteer
• Kept patients comfortable by providing assistance with personal care
• Communicated with nursing staff about patient needs

EDUCATION AND CERTIFICATION
Associate of Science in Nursing Assistance degree, Marabou University, Boston, MA, 2017
Massachusetts Nurse Aide Registry—Current
CPR and First Aid, American Heart Association, Boston, MA, 2017

OTHER SKILLS
• Familiar with medical terminology and disease control standards
• Fluent in Spanish

This example shows a résumé for a certified nursing assistant position. It has an easy-to-read format that highlights the applicant's experience, education, and skills.

When interviewing for a health care job, it is important to dress professionally and be cordial and respectful to all those you meet. Be sure to display a positive attitude to show the interviewer that you would be a good person to work with daily.

If you speak a language other than English, state this as well. With the vast numbers of non-English-speaking patients in the health care system, being bilingual can be a major advantage when applying for a job.

Be sure to proofread your résumé—or better yet, have someone else read it. Those working in the health care field must be detail-oriented and careful. A résumé with mistakes in it creates the wrong impression.

INTERVIEWING FOR A WOMEN'S HEALTH CARE JOB

The interview is your opportunity to convince a prospective employer to hire you. Before going to an interview, look up the company on the internet. This research allows you to demonstrate that you understand what the facility does and explain how your training and skills apply.

Dress professionally in neat, clean clothing and be well groomed. Speak respectfully, using correct grammar. You may be asked about experience or skills you don't have; explain how your education or experience in other areas equips you to learn those skills. Often interviewers ask questions designed to see how applicants react under stress or analyze problems. Practice answering difficult questions, such as "What are your weaknesses?" in advance. That way you can answer them fluently when asked.

If you are young and have little experience, you may be asked whether you will be responsible, show up on time, and perform tasks when you are not supervised. Be ready with examples of times when you were expected to carry out an activity or look after others and did so responsibly. Be sure to be polite to everyone you meet because the interviewer will be evaluating applicants' people skills as well as their practical ones.

ADVANCING YOUR CAREER

It is possible to start with an entry- or mid-level job and advance to a higher-level position by undertaking additional training and education. One option is to continue your education part-time while you work. In many cases, employers provide tuition reimbursement for those continuing their education in the field. Some hospitals and medical centers allow employees to take training programs offered by the facility, for free or at a reduced rate.

Those who start out as licensed practical nurses can expand their education by obtaining a bachelor's degree in nursing and becoming RNs. RNs with associate's degrees can convert them to bachelor's degrees through additional

The woman's health care field offers excellent opportunities to advance in one's career, for example from RN to nurse practitioner.

education. Nurses interested in becoming nurse managers, nursing supervisors, or educators can study for advanced degrees. RNs can become specialty nurses or nurse practitioners. Technologists who obtain advanced degrees can become laboratory managers. Medical assistants can undertake additional training to become physician assistants.

Thus, the careers described here can provide both a fulfilling job and lifelong career opportunities.

glossary

accredited Authorized, or given approval, by a recognized organization.

adept Skilled.

Alzheimer's disease An age-related decline in brain function.

ambulation Moving around or walking about.

anatomy The structure of the body.

cervix The neck of the womb.

cesarean section A method of removing a baby through a surgical cut in the walls of the abdomen and womb; also called a C-section.

chronic Going on for a long time.

critical care unit A section of a hospital that houses patients who are extremely ill.

cystic fibrosis An inherited disease that causes the body to make mucus that is very thick and sticky. It generally appears in early childhood and causes serious difficulty in breathing and digesting food.

day-surgery unit A section of a hospital in which patients undergo surgery and then return home on the same day.

disproportionate Unequal, having more influence than would be expected.

fetus An unborn baby.

fibromyalgia A chronic condition that causes pain in the muscles and joints and can lead to sleep and mood disorders.

GED General Education Diploma or General Equivalency Diploma, a credential earned by a person who did not graduate from high school that certifies that the person has passed tests showing that he or she has the same academic skills as someone who graduated from an American or Canadian high school.

genitalia The sex organs.

hormone A chemical produced in the body that regulates bodily functions.

intensive care unit The section of a hospital that houses the most desperately ill or injured patients and those at high risk of complications from surgery.

menstrual Related to getting one's period.

millennial A person born between about 1982 and 2000.

neonatal Newborn.

obstetrical Relating to pregnancy and childbirth.

oncology The study of cancer.

osteoporosis A medical condition in which bones become weak and brittle, causing them to break or fracture easily.

ovaries The organs in a women's body that contain and release eggs.

physiology The study of the processes that take place in the body.

psychopharmacologist A psychiatrist who specializes in prescribing medication for patients with psychological problems.

recovery room An area where patients are taken temporarily for monitoring when they leave the operating room after surgery.

resident A doctor who is in the final stages of medical training.

sickle-cell disease An inherited red blood cell condition. Red blood cells become hard and sticky and have the shape of the letter C, like a sickle, which is a farm tool with a curved blade that is used for cutting.

step-down facility A place that a patient is sent to from a hospital that provides more care than can be provided at home but less than at a hospital, such as a nursing home or rehabilitation center.

sterile Free of germs.

stigma A sign of disgrace; a negative effect on a person's reputation.

Tay-Sachs disease An inherited disease that is caused by a missing enzyme that leads to the accumulation of a fatty substance in nerve cells in the brain. It is a progressive condition and is fatal in early childhood.

uterus The organ in a woman's body where a fetus is carried.

vital signs Basic measures of body function, such as pulse, blood pressure, and temperature.

for more information

American Association of Medical Assistants (AAMA)
20 N. Wacker Drive, Suite 1575
Chicago, IL 60606
(312) 899-1500 or (800) 228-2262
Website: http://www.aama-ntl.org
Facebook: @aamaorg
Twitter: @AAMAOfficial
AAMA provides certification for medical assistants and a
    website that includes educational information, network-
    ing, and news.

American College of Nurse Midwives (ACNM)
8403 Colesville Road, Suite 500
Silver Spring, MD 20910
(240) 485-1800
Website: http://www.midwife.org
Facebook: @ACNMmidwives
Twitter: @ACNMmidwives
ACNM provides midwifery training, certification, and job-
    hunting resources.

American Counseling Association (ACA)
6101 Stevenson Avenue
Alexandria, VA 22304
(703) 823-9800
Website: https://www.counseling.org
Facebook: @American.Counseling.Association
The ACA provides information, career assistance, a variety of
    books and journals, and a newsletter for counselors.

American Registry of Radiological Technicians (ARRT)
1255 Northland Drive
St. Paul, MN 55120-1155
(651) 687-0048
Website: https://www.arrt.org
Facebook: @americanregistryofradiologictechnologists
The ARRT provides certification for radiological technicians
in fifteen disciplines. Its website includes information for
students about credentials in medical imaging, certain
procedures, and radiation therapy.

Bureau of Labor Statistics (BLS)
Postal Square Building
2 Massachusetts Avenue NE
Washington, DC 20212
(202) 691-5200
Website: http://www.bls.gov
Facebook: @departmentoflabor
Twitter: BLS_gov
The Bureau of Labor Statistics is an agency within the US
Department of Labor dedicated to gathering data about
the labor market, working conditions, and the career
outlook for many jobs. Each year, the BLS updates the
Occupational Outlook Handbook (http://www.bls.gov
/ooh/), which provides information about thousands of
careers, job requirements, and average salaries.

Canadian Association of Midwives (CAM)
2330 rue Notre-Dame Ouest, Suite 300
Montréal, QC H3J 1N4
Canada
(514) 807-3668
Website: http://www.canadianmidwives.org

Facebook: @CanadianMidwives
Twitter: @CanadianMidwives
CAM offers information on midwife training programs, news
    of interest to midwives, and a journal.

Canadian Society for Medical Laboratory Science (CSMLS)
33 Wellington Street North
Hamilton, ON L8R 1M7
Canada
(800) 263-8277
Website: http://www.csmls.org
Facebook: @csmls
Twitter: @csmls
This organization provides certification of medical laboratory
    assistants and technologists. It also provides resources
    including medical news and a job bank.

Cardiovascular Credentialing International (CCI)
1500 Sunday Drive, Suite 102
Raleigh, NC 27607
(800) 325-0268
Website: http://www.cci-online.org
This organization provides education and certification for
    cardiovascular technologists. Its website includes informa-
    tion about its programs and events, as well as job listings.

Childbirth and Postpartum Professional Association (CAPPA)
PO Box 547
Flowery Branch, GA 30542
(770) 965-9777
Website: http://www.icappa.net
Facebook: @CAPPAnetworking
Twitter: @CAPPAnetworking
Instagram: @CAPPAnetworking

CAPPA is an international training and certification organization for doulas and childbirth educators.

National Council on the State Boards of Nursing (NCSBN)
111 East Wacker Drive, Suite 2900
Chicago, IL 60601-4277
(312) 525-3600
Website: http://www.ncsbn.org
Facebook: @NCSBNOfficial
Twitter: @NCSBN
This organization provides licensing exams for various levels of nurses. It also provides a variety of publications and online courses.

Society of Diagnostic Medical Sonography (SDMS)
2745 Dallas Parkway, Suite 350
Plano, TX 75093-8730
(800) 229-9506
Website: http://www.sdms.org
Facebook: @SDMS3
Twitter: @TheSDMS
The SDMS provides resources, including a scientific journal and a newsletter, for ultrasound technologists.

WEBSITES

Because of the changing nature of internet links, Rosen Publishing has developed an online list of websites related to the subject of this book. This site is updated regularly. Please use this link to access the list:

http://www.rosenlinks.com/ECAR/Women

for further reading

Bickerstaff, Linda. *What Degree Do I Need to Pursue a Career in Nursing?* (The Right Degree for Me). New York, NY: Rosen Publishing, 2015.

Brezina, Corona. *Getting a Job in Health Care* (Job Basics: Getting the Job You Need). New York, NY: Rosen Publishing, 2014.

Christen, Carol, and Richard N. Bolles. *What Color Is Your Parachute? for Teens: Discover Yourself, Design Your Future, and Plan for Your Dream Job.* 3rd ed. Berkeley, CA: Ten Speed Press, 2016.

Ehrenreich, Barbara, and Deirdre English. *Witches, Midwives, and Nurses: A History of Women Healers.* 2nd ed. New York, NY: The Feminist Press, 2010.

Gerdin, Judith A. *Health Careers Today.* 6th ed. St. Louis, MO: Elsevier, 2017.

Job Readiness for Health Professionals: Soft Skill Strategies for Success. 2nd ed. St. Louis, MO: Elsevier/Saunders, 2016.

Johnson, Anne. *Medical and Clinical Laboratory Technologist Career: The Insider's Guide to Finding a Job at an Amazing Firm, Acing the Interview & Getting Promoted.* Special ed. CreateSpace Publishing, 2016.

Rodriguez Ohanesian, Jessi. *The Ultimate Guide to the Physician Assistant Profession.* New York, NY: McGraw-Hill, 2014.

Simons, Rae. *Nurse* (Careers with Character). Broomall, PA: Mason Crest Publishers, 2014.

Smoker, Annabel. *Launching Your Career in Nursing and Midwifery: A Practical Guide.* Ebook. New York, NY: Palgrave Macmillan, 2016.

Wittner, Seth. *True Tales from a Physician's Assistant.* CreateSpace Publishing, 2015.

bibliography

Alexander, Linda Lewis, Judith H. LaRosa, Helaine Bader, Susan Garfield, and William James Alexander. *New Dimensions in Women's Health*. Burlington, MA 2014.

Counselor-License. "Types of Counselors." Retrieved March 7, 2017. http://www.counselor-license.com/articles /types-of-counselors.html#context/api/listings/prefilter.

Dali, Timothy M., Ritashree Chakrabarti, Michael V. Storm, Erika C. Elwell, and William F. Rayburn. "Estimated Demand for Women's Health Services by 2020." *Journal of Women's Health*, July 22, 2013. https://www.ncbi.nlm.nih .gov/pmc/articles/PMC3704110.

Dewitt, Neal. "The Transition from Home to Hospital Birth." *Birth*. Vol. 4, Issue 2 (1997): 47.

ExploreHealthCareers.org. "Nurses Aid/Assistant." Retrieved March 4, 2017. https://explorehealthcareers.org/career /allied-health-professions/nurses-aide.

Feldhusen, Adrian A. "The History of Midwifery and Childbirth in America: A Time Line." *Midwifery Today*. Retrieved March 5, 2017. https://www.midwiferytoday .com/articles/timeline.asp.

Health Jobs Start Here. "Internships & Volunteering." Retrieved March 6, 2017. http://www.healthjobsstarthere .com/resources/experience/find.

Health Jobs Start Here. "Scholarships & Financial Aid." Retrieved January 6, 2013. http://www.health-jobsstarthere.com/resources/financial/scholarships.

Kintz, Jennifer. "What Being a Medical Assistant Is All About." AllAlliedHealthSchools.com. Retrieved March 7, 2017. http://www.allalliedhealthschools.com/health -careers/medical-assisting/being-a-medicalassistant.

Mark, Joshua J. "Female Physicians in Ancient Egypt." *Ancient History Encyclopedia*, February 22, 2017. http:// www.ancient.eu/article/49.

Morkes, Andrew. *Hot Health Care Careers: 30 Occupations with Fast Growth and Many New Job Openings*. Chicago, IL: College & Career Press, 2017.

Nurse Journal. "Requirements to Become a Nurse Practitioner." Retrieved March 15, 2017. http://nursejournal.org/nurse-practitioner/what-to-know -to-become-a-nurse-practitioner.Practice Quiz. "Certified Professional Midwife Exam Prep." Retrieved March 22, 2017. https://www.practicequiz.com/question/12388.

Sadr, Allison. "History of Midwifery." Dimensions Healthcare System. Retrieved March 13, 2017. https://www.dimensionshealth.org/dimensions-health -services-prince-georges-county-maryland-md/midwifery /history-of-midwifery.

Sanghani, Radhika. "What Is It Actually Like to Be a Midwife Today?" *Telegraph*, March 11, 2014. http://www .telegraph.co.uk/women/mother-tongue/10668429 /What-is-it-actually-like-to-be-a-midwife-today.html.

Turner, Susan Odegaard. *Healthcare Career Guide*. Amazon Digital Services, 2013.

US Department of Labor. Bureau of Labor Statistics. "Healthcare Occupations." *Occupational Outlook Handbook*, December 17, 2015. https://www.bls.gov/ooh /healthcare/home.htm.

Villanova University. "Job Outlook for Registered Nurses (RN)." Retrieved March 13, 2017. https://www.villanovau.com/resources/nursing/registered -nurse-rn-job-description/#.WMao__nyuUk.

index

B

birth control, 9, 13
birthing
    at home, 41, 45, 56
    at a hospital, 43, 45
birth trainer, 56
Blackwell, Eizabeth, 9

C

careers in patient assistance
    certified home health aide, 52
    personal care aide, 51–52
    social service aide, 50
certified home health aides, 52
certified midwives (CMs), 45, 46, 47
certified nurse-midwives (CNMs),
    11, 45, 46, 47
certified nursing assistants (CNAs),
    25, 27
certified professional midwives
    (CPMs), 45, 49
childbed fever, 43
child care, 58
counselor
    education needed to be a, 57
    types of, 56–58
critical care nurses, 31–33

D

doula, 56

E

endocrinologists, 13, 38

F

family planning, 12, 16, 37

G

geneticists, 13, 38, 40
gynecological disease, 7
gynecological oncologists, 38

H

health insurance, 6
Hippocrates, 7

I

interviewing for a job, 62, 64–65

K

Kahun Gynecological Papyrus, 7

L

labor and delivery nurses, 33
lab technician
    clinical, 54–55
    education and training to be a, 55
licensed practical nurses (LPNs),
    27–28

M

medical assistants, 55–56
midwife
certification exam, 47
certified (CM), 45, 46, 47
certified nurse-midwife (CNM),
11, 45, 46, 47
certified professional (CPM), 45, 49
midwifery
history of, 41, 43, 45
profession of, 45
training and certification, 24, 46,
47, 49

N

neonatal critical care nurses, 33
nurse anesthetists, 31
nurses in women's health care
certified nursing assistant (CNA),
25, 27
education, 22–23
licensed practical (LPN), 27–28
registered (RN), 28, 30
specialty, 31, 33
nurse practitioners, 36, 66

O

OBGYNs, 37
obstetrics, 11, 12, 34, 35, 43, 45

P

personal care aides, 51–52
physician assistants, 36, 66
pregnancy, 7, 12, 13, 37, 45, 54, 56
public health, 16, 31, 58–59, 62

R

registered nurses (RNs), 28, 30
résumés, 60, 62–64

S

Sanger, Margaret, 9
Semmelweis, Ignaz, 43
social service aides, 50
surgical nurses, 33

T

technologists
cardiovascular, 52, 53
electroencephalogram, 53–54
radiological, 54
sonographer, 54
Trota of Salerno, 9

W

women's doctor
becoming a, 34–35
specialties as a, 36, 37–38, 40
women's health advocacy, 57
women's health care
in ancient Egypt, 7
and cancer, 12, 13, 36, 37, 38, 40,
54
history of, 7, 9–10
in the Middle Ages, 9
practice of, 25, 27, 28, 31, 33,
34–38
specialties in, 10, 12–14, 15, 16
women's health career
advancing in a, 65–66
assistance for training in, 30–31

certification and licensing for, 24
education for, 22–23
in endocrinology and genetics, 13, 35, 38
in fertility and infertility treat-ment, 12, 35–36, 37
finding a, 60, 61, 62,
in gerontology, 14
high school preparation for, 18–19, 21
in home health care, 27, 50, 51, 52, 60
interviewing for, 64–65
as a medical assistant, 55–56
in mental health and substance abuse specialists, 13–14, 56,
in nursing, 25, 27–28, 30, 31–32
in nutrition and weight manage-ment, 12–13
as surgeons and rehabilitation experts, 13, 38,
as technologists, 52–55
women's liberation movement, 10

ABOUT THE AUTHOR

Jeri Freedman has a BA from Harvard University. She has more than fifteen years of experience in sales and marketing for high-tech and medical products companies, including the clinical assays division of Baxter-Travenol. She is the author of numerous young adult nonfiction books, including *Careers in Emergency Medical Response Teams' Search and Rescue Units*; *Women in the Workplace: Wages, Respect, and Equal Rights*; *Being a Leader: Organizing and Inspiring a Group*; *Jumpstarting a Career in Hospitals & Home Health Care*; *Careers in Pharmaceutical Sales*; and *Careers in Human Resources*. She has also written books on brain cancer, ovarian cancer, thyroid cancer, and hepatitis B. She lives in Boston, Massachusetts.

PHOTO CREDITS

Design: Matt Cauli; Layout: Tahara Anderson; Senior Editor: Kathy Kuhtz Campbell; Photo Research: Karen Huang